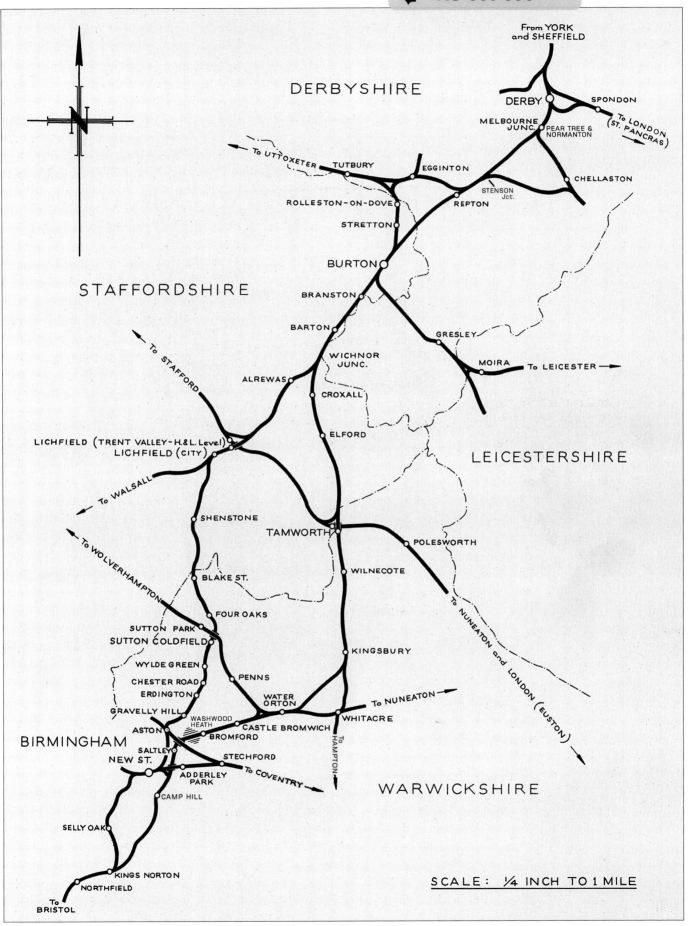

Derby, summer 1957. The Midland Railway regularly diagrammed 0-6-0 freight engines on excursion and relief passenger trains, a tradition which carried on into BR days. But in summer 1957 it was impressive to see 9F 2-10-0s being used on such duties. 92051 makes a smoky departure from Derby station heading towards Birmingham on a summer Saturday relief from the north-east, while a Midland 2P 4-4-0, 40416, shunts in the background.

P J Lynch

Introduction

George Stephenson, who had been engaged to survey the route in 1834, reported to the Birmingham & Derby Junction Railway committee in April 1835 that he 'saw no difficulty in constructing a line from Derby and suggested a junction with the London to Birmingham Railway at Stechford. By this trains might use that company's Birmingham station. As this station might also be used by the Birmingham & Gloucester Railway there could be opportunities for interchange of traffic. A branch from the main line at Whitacre to a second junction with the London & Birmingham at Hampton could be used for interchange with traffic bound for London'.

The Birmingham and Derby Railway (B&D) opened for traffic on 12 August 1839 and the two-hour trip was along a different route from today's journey between these two Midlands cities. B&D trains set off south-east from the London & Birmingham Railway's Curzon Street station, steaming along the L&B's London line via Stechford to Hampton-in-Arden. There, B&D services reversed and went north to Whitacre, Tamworth, Burton on Trent and a temporary station at Derby. In those early days, trains from London to the north, operated by B&D locomotives, traversed Hampton, Whitacre and Derby before competing lines, such as the Midland Counties Railway, opened in 1840 and took away most of the traffic. The Midland Counties brought down the distance from London to Derby via Rugby to 130 miles, whereas it was 141 miles via Hampton-in-Arden and the B&D.

The original B&D Act of Parliament authorised a railway direct from Stechford to Whitacre, with the section from Whitacre to Hampton intended as a branch. Sharing the L&B line as far as Hampton was unsatisfactory, so after trains had commenced operating between Birmingham and Derby, the B&D directors applied to cancel the as yet unbuilt section from Stechford, and instead construct their own station in Birmingham and a new, completely independent, route to Whitacre along the River Tame valley. The proposed Birmingham station was to terminate a stone's throw from the Curzon Street terminus of the L&B and the Grand Junction Railway to Liverpool and Manchester. Thus from 10 February 1842 Derby-bound passenger services left the B&D's new station at Lawley Street and travelled to Whitacre via

Castle Bromwich, Water Orton and Forge Mills, with goods trains following this routing from 11 April and mail trains from 1 July 1842. At Derby, the B&D connected with the Midland Counties Railway, which went east to Leicester, and the North Midland Railway, north to Leeds. All three companies – which formed the Midland Railway in 1844 – used the joint station, opened on 11 May 1840 and built by the North Midland Railway on land purchased by the B&D. At the Birmingham end, passenger services for Derby and the north were transferred back to Curzon Street from 1 May 1851, utilising a new spur from Landor Street Junction to 'Derby Junction'; Lawley Street was developed into a first class goods depot. From 1 July 1854 some Midland Railway passenger trains started using the LNWR's new central station in Birmingham, at New Street, resulting in the closure of Curzon Street to regular passenger traffic. So passengers for Derby over the fifteen year period would have used three different stations to depart from Birmingham! However through trains between Derby and Bristol still tended to bypass New Street due to the necessity for a reversal and continued to use the old Birmingham & Gloucester Railway Camp Hill route.

As a result of congestion at New Street the Midland spent £1/2 million on enlargements in the 1880s which involved building another station similar in size to the existing one, to the south of Great Queen Street which became a central carriage road. Some MR services started to use the new station from February 1885 while through workings were added in October that year when the Birmingham West Suburban Railway from King's Norton and Bournville was extended into New Street with construction of the line from Church Road. The station started to operate as two with the LNWR using the 'Old Station' and the MR the newly opened 'Extension Station'.

From October 1889, all MR passenger trains used the new side. But the Midland was still utilising running powers over LNWR tracks to gain access into New Street from Derby Junction, so it constructed its own independent approach through an underpass line from Derby Junction to Grand Junction and a new south tunnel, opened for traffic from May 1896.

Contents

Birmingham New Street. A birds-eye view of the old New Street, with the ex-LNWR station prominent under its arched roof and the more modest Midland Railway part on the right-hand side of Queen's Drive. This picture shows the wonderful curve of the roof. Trams clatter along Navigation Street, with a motor bus in view as well. Tracks from the Midland side are at the bottom right of the picture. The overall roof on the Midland side survived World War 2, unlike that of the North-Western part of the station.

Above: **New Street, 1949.** 'Royal Scot' 4-6-0s became common on the Birmingham-Derby route in the early 1960s when they were at sheds like Saltley and Derby following dieselisation of their duties elsewhere. But 46120 *Royal Inniskilling Fusilier* was a bit of a novelty standing at platform 9 on the Midland side in 1949 under the elevated No. 4 signal cabin. It had a short period allocated to 17A Derby and worked trains between York and Bristol. The same loco also spent time at Derby Test Centre and the shed in 1955. *HMRS*

Below: **New Street, 22 June 1963.** The Midland side, Derby end, is displayed, with signal cabin 2 prominent. Platforms from right to left are 7, 8, 9,10, with 11 just visible. The occasional shaft of light penetrates the gloom of the interior. *R K Blencowe collection*

Above: **New Street, 8 August 1964.** A rare engine without doubt is ex-LNER Pacific 60114 *W P Allen*. It is all steamed up ready for departure on the 11.41am relief for Newcastle. Appearance of the loco here was connected with an enthusiast rail tour which it worked into the area. Another sighting of an LNER Pacific at New Street was on 24 January 1963 when the 8.20am Newcastle-Swansea was hauled from Derby to Birmingham by no less than A3 60039 *Sandwich* of 34A King's Cross.   *T J Edgington*

Below: **New Street, 22 April 1965.** Soon the old New Street would be swept away with contracts let in 1964 for a complete rebuilding of the station in six stages. This view is eastwards under the footbridge, which passed above all the platforms, and along Queen's Drive. The new station opened on 6 March 1967.   *B W L Brooksbank*

Grand Junction, 18 August 1949. Grand Junction is one of the great names in British railway history. The picture is from the Grand Junction signal box opened in April 1896 to control the now quadruple main lines. The ex-LMS 0-6-0T is on the line to Banbury Street wharf. As for the main lines the left hand pair are the down and up (to Derby) Midland. Next are the down and up (to London) ex-LNWR lines. Tracks under the elevated LNW line to Bescot and Walsall enter the ex-LNW Curzon Street goods yard and depot. Another famous name, Proof House Junction box can be discerned in the middle distance. To the rear of this view, the two Midland lines split to become the down and up Derby and Gloucester lines, while Exchange Sidings existed to transfer traffic between the LNWR and MR.

J H L Adams, Kidderminster Railway Museum

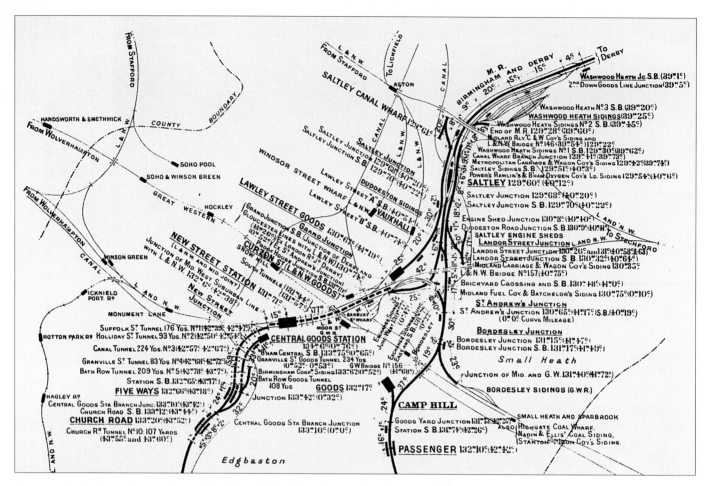

Below: **St Andrew's Junction, 21 July 1978.** Dieselisation did not end the need for banking. Brush Co-Co 47339 heads a loaded train of merry-go-round coal hoppers towards Camp Hill leaving the Saltley line with a banker visible in the background. Compared with steam days, modernisation had also introduced air braking and got rid of brake vans. The lines on the left go towards Grand Junction and New Street.
M Mensing

Above: **St Andrew's Junction, 1962**. The original Birmingham & Gloucester line curved round from Grand Junction and carried on through Camp Hill to King's Norton and the west of England. At Landor Street Junction was a connection with the Birmingham & Derby line; this Camp Hill route was heavily used for freight as well as some passenger trains which avoided the congestion at New Street station, particularly on summer Saturdays. The gradients meant that bankers were used as required and 4F 43958 is seen providing assistance to a freight. *N Preedy*

Below: **Camp Hill, 8 July 1936**. A glimpse of the old order as 3F 0-6-0 3441 of Gloucester shed, 22B, blowing off mightily, storms through on a westbound freight, probably from Washwood Heath.

L W Perkins, Kidderminster Railway Museum

Lawley Street Goods Depot, c.1907. The Midland Railway opened a large goods and grain warehouse here in 1895 adjacent to Grand Junction and at the end of a 1200 yard branch from Duddeston Road Junction, near Saltley. The goods shed covered two and a half acres. This magnificent view shows the typically busy goods yard. A horse-drawn vehicle awaits its next duty, while a Johnson 0-6-0T shunts alongside Lawley Street 'B' signal box.

Roy F Burrows Midland Collection Trust, Derby Industrial Museum

Above: **Landor Street Junction, 1957.** A view from the signal box shows 4F 44413 heading off on the Camp Hill line with a freight for Gloucester while the Birmingham to Derby route is over on the left. Lawley Street 'A' box is in the background. Saltley shed coaling tower is on the right. *R S Carpenter collection*

Below: **Saltley loco depot, September 1936.** Saltley was big and rightly famed for its large allocation of 0-6-0 freight engines, though it also had some notable passenger turns and engines. The original Birmingham & Derby engine shed very quickly proved inadequate for the Midland Railway, so a round house was built at Saltley in the 1850s with a 39 foot turntable. This accomodation was soon outgrown and a new site was identified on the other side of the main line; eventually the Midland Railway had no less than three sheds in use at Saltley plus an eight-road fitting shop. The shed code in Midland days was '3' but became the more familiar 21A in the 1930s. In this view things look pretty quiet, but no doubt there were lots of locos lurking in the roundhouses. The concrete coaling plant was built in this year having a capacity of 300 tons of coal. It replaced a standard MR coaling shed which must have caused delays due to the sheer number of engines needing to be serviced.

Saltley loco depot. Two views inside the roundhouses show various loco types. The top picture was taken on 6 June 1948 when the locos all display LMS front numbers. 493 and 4920 were Saltley allocated, while 8635 hailed from Nottingham and 4804 from Bristol. The lower view is dated 15 September 1963, the month that Saltley was recoded 2E from the long-familiar 21A whose engines would, it often seemed, turn up in the most unlikely corners of BR. Saltley closed to steam in March 1967, though the site remained as a diesel depot.

Roger Shenton; Joe Moss collection, R S Carpenter

Above: **Saltley Junction, 5 August 1962**. The Saltley area was ripe with the aromas of smoke and steam mixing with the odours of a more pungent variety from gas works and other industries. The atmosphere of the area is captured in this shot of 44814 on a class 'D' part-fitted express freight. *B W L Brooksbank, Initial Photographs*

Below: **Saltley, 5 July 1947**. 'Crab' 2-6-0 2903 of 21A passes Saltley Sidings box and approaches Saltley station on a local passenger working, with the gas holder looming over the scene. *F W Shuttleworth*

Above: **Saltley, 25 October 1964**. A view of the station. The original opened in 1854, but was replaced in 1899. It closed to all traffic on and from 4 March 1968. Saltley was not the closest station to the loco shed however; that was Vauxhall & Duddeston on the LNW line to Bescot which was 5 minutes walk, whereas from here it was 10 minutes.

R J Essery collection

Below: **Washwood Heath, 27 April 1957**. 2F 0-6-0 58261 engages in some shunting under the bridge carrying the ex-LNW line between Stafford, Aston, Stechford, Hampton-in-Arden and Rugby. *B W L Brooksbank*

Above: **Washwood Heath, 25 October 1964.** Seen here on the down side are the pilot sidings for shunting locos and bankers of Camp Hill bound freights. The start of the extensive Washwood Heath down side yards and No.2 signal box is glimpsed beyond the bridge. The road bridge over the MR lines then goes under the LNW line.

R J Essery collection

Below: **CEGB Nechells.** Many of the industrial concerns alongside the Birmingham-Derby line had their own locomotives for internal shunting and exchanging traffic with BR. The likes of Metro-Cammell had gone over to diesels by the 1960s, but quite a number of steam locos could be seen at places such as West Midlands Gas Board and the Central Electricity Generating Board at Nechells; Stewarts & Lloyds, Bromford Tube Works; Dunlop Rubber Co, Fort Dunlop, while the CEGB Hams Hall power station complex had no less than ten steam locos. At Nechells power station, a Robert Stephenson & Hawthorns 0-6-0T shunts wagons to and from BR's exchange sidings near Washwood Heath marshalling yards. This loco type also predominated at Hams Hall.

S Mourton

Washwood Heath, March 1905.

Washwood Heath was an ideal place for the expanding Midland Railway to develop sorting sidings. Although close to the rivers Rea and the Tame, the greenfield land was flat. With junctions to major parts of the Midland network – north to Walsall, east to Leicester and south to Lawley Street and central Birmingham, this was a good site on its Derby to Bristol route. It also boasted links to the GWR and LNWR close by. This magnificent official Midland Railway portrait shows the down yard. The down sidings were first opened in October 1877, enlarged in 1891, with further expansion in 1935. The up yard and sidings came into use in January 1918, with more added in 1930. When they were completed, both sides were 'hump' shunted. This involved the engine being detached from an arrivals train. Next, the complete train would be dragged backwards to a shunting neck. The train was then 'cut' into groups of wagons or single ones according to their destination. Shunters literally chased the wagons as they came off the hump to pin down the brakes using long shunting poles to give extra leverage. In the dark winter nights, especially during the war-time blackout conditions, this must have been a very hazardous job. By this process trains of wagons were assembled and tripped to various destinations like Central Goods depot and Lawley Street (MR), Curzon Street and Exchange sidings (LNWR), Bordesley (GWR) as well as various other local sites. In the up direction trains were assembled similarly. So the area contained a huge marshalling complex for many years which survived the end of steam, but gradually ran down from the late 1960s.

National Railway Museum/
Science & Society Picture Library

Washwood Heath (WWH). On the down side were: WWH Sidings No.2 seen on 8 April 1969; WWH Sidings No. 3 on 5 April 1969; WWH Sidings No. 4 photographed on 31 October 1971. At the Bromford Bridge end of the complex was Washwood Heath Junction box, observed from a passing train on 12 April 1969.   *M A King*

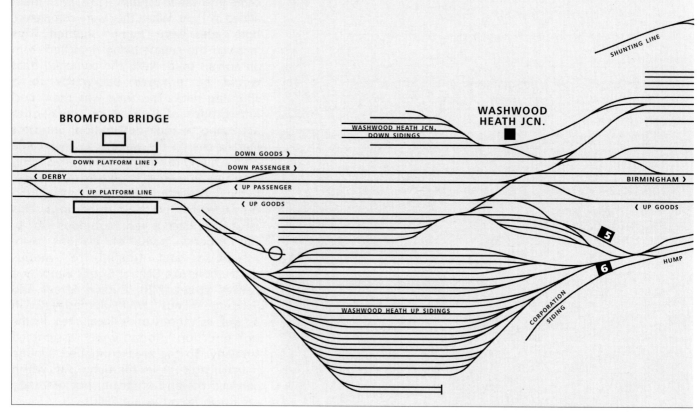

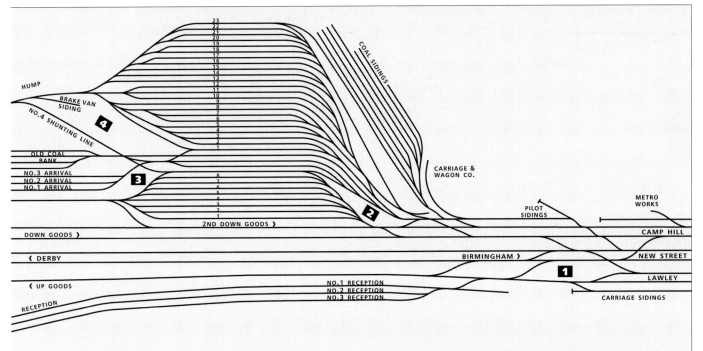

Labels on diagram:

23 22 21 20 19 18 17 16 15 14 13 12 11 10 9 8 7 6 5 4 3 2 1

HUMP

BRAKE VAN SIDING

4

NO.4 SHUNTING LINE

OLD COAL BANK

NO.3 ARRIVAL
NO.2 ARRIVAL
NO.1 ARRIVAL

3

8 7 6 5 4 3 2 1

2ND DOWN GOODS ⟩

DOWN GOODS ⟩

⟨ DERBY

⟨ UP GOODS

RECEPTION

COAL SIDINGS

CARRIAGE & WAGON CO.

2

PILOT SIDINGS

METRO WORKS

CAMP HILL

BIRMINGHAM ⟩

1

NEW STREET

LAWLEY

CARRIAGE SIDINGS

NO.1 RECEPTION
NO.2 RECEPTION
NO.3 RECEPTION

Washwood Heath. On the way out of Birmingham, three boxes were located on the up side at Washwood Heath: WWH Sidings No 1 seen on 25 October 1964 *R J Essery collection*; WWH Sidings No. 5 on 17 November 1973 *M A King*; WWH Sidings No. 6 on 5 April 1969 *M A King*.

Left, above: **Washwood Heath, 5 September 1962.** With Nechells power station looming over the scene, 2-6-0 42855 trundles a parcels train past the exit from Washwood Heath up yard, which has a goodly number of wagons in view. *B W L Brooksbank*

Left, below: **Bromford Bridge.** Nearby was this station, which is portrayed in a positively bucolic setting, after all the heavy industry encountered on the way out of Birmingham. The station opened in 1896 on the site of the short-lived Bromford Forge station of the 1840s and was normally only used on race days when many specials would be run to here. The platforms were located on the goods lines and special block posts were brought into operation at Bromford Bridge South and North for the race trains. Closure was effected in June 1965, but there is pressure to have a station here once more. *Stations UK*

Below: **Bromford Bridge, 5 September 1962.** Bromford Bridge is a lot more industrial in this later view as 4F 44180 passes with an up goods and another loco is shunting the sidings. There was a fuel storage depot for the Esso Petroleum Company here and at this date it was the destination for several heavy tanker trains each weekday from various places including Avonmouth Docks and Fawley Refinery, near Southampton, originally diagrammed for 9F 2-10-0s, with the latter trains also seeing Southern Region class 33 diesels. *B W L Brooksbank*

LMS
LONDON MIDLAND AND SCOTTISH RAILWAY

BIRMINGHAM STEEPLECHASES

FIRST RACE, 1.30 p.m.   LAST RACE, 4.0 p.m. each day.

NOTE.—The Electric Totalisator will operate at this Meeting.

On MONDAY & TUESDAY
February 15th & 16th, 1932
Special Trains
FROM
BIRMINGHAM (New Street) to
BROMFORD BRIDGE
(RACECOURSE STATION)

at 12.10, 12A50 and 1.5 p.m.

RETURN FARE. Birmingham to Bromford Bridge and back.	SPECIAL REDUCED FARES THIRD CLASS.	SINGLE FARE. Bromford Bridge to Birmingham only.
1/-	← →	8d.

CHILDREN under three years of age, free; three years and under fourteen, half-fares.

"A."—This train will start from KING'S NORTON at 12.30 p.m., calling at Selly Oak 12.35 p.m. Return Fares to Bromford Bridge:—From King's Norton 1/8, Selly Oak 1/5.

RETURN ARRANGEMENTS.

Passengers return on day of issue only from BROMFORD BRIDGE at 4.15 p.m., 4.35 p.m or 4.55 p.m.

NOTE.—The 4.15 p.m. train from Bromford Bridge is a through train to Birmingham (New Street), Selly Oak and King's Norton.

PLEASE RETAIN THIS BILL FOR REFERENCE.

FOR CONDITIONS, ETC., SEE OVER.

7,250 H., 96 P.   Bemrose & Sons Ltd., Derby and London.

Castle Bromwich , 3 June 1925. The goods lines pass round the outside of the station platforms where this superb picture of a Midland express with 2P 4-4-0 531, complete with brakes on the bogie wheels and coal rails to increase the capacity of the tender, was taken. The leading vehicle is a 12-wheel bogie restaurant car; the Midland was justly proud of the comfort, service and food provided.

W L Good

Above: **Castle Bromwich, May 1910**. The station building in Midland Railway days and dating from 1901, although the station first opened in 1842 at the behest of local landowner the Earl of Bradford. Local services pausing here ran from Birmingham to Derby and Leicester via Nuneaton, also to Walsall via Sutton Park. A few expresses such as the Worcester to York also called. Even after local passengers ceased to stop here in March 1968, excursion trains continued to call.

Below: **Castle Bromwich**. This was the site of part of the British Industries Fair which was a huge international trade event for many years. Giving the lie to the alleged insularity of the English, the sign 'Alight Here For The Fair' is shown in four languages! A Caprotti valve gear 'Black Five' adds its own international flavour as it steams through on an up express for the Derby line.   *R S Carpenter collection*

Above: **Castle Bromwich, May 1957.** With Castle Bromwich signal box in the background ex-works 3F 43194 takes a freight from Derby to King's Norton. 43194 had been built at Derby in 1896, not for the Midland Railway, but for the Somerset & Dorset. It was taken over, along with all the other S&D locos, by the LMS in 1930. Note the sandpipe located near the front buffer beam, apparently all 'native' S&D 0-6-0s had extra sanders front and back, compared with their MR/LMS sisters. 43194 was working home to 71H Templecombe on the S&D, but somewhere *en route* got a hot box, as it was languishing on Gloucester Barnwood shed by 19 May, with the centre driving wheels missing – these having been returned to Derby Works for repair! *Real Photographs*

Below: **Castle Bromwich, 7 July 1962.** From a Southern Region based loco to one from the Eastern. The daily Cleethorpes to Birmingham New Street passenger train had for some years regularly brought a 'B1' 4-6-0 along the line through Castle Bromwich and the honour falls to 61318 on this occasion. The train ran via Leicester, Nuneaton and Whitacre. By the date of this picture, 'B1s' had in fact become quite common, with a good number based at Sheffield which often worked trains via Derby and Birmingham down to Bristol and even Bath. While the train occupies the down fast line it has just passed over the pointwork for a pair of lines heading north from Castle Bromwich Junction to Park Lane Junction and Walsall. *R J Buckley*

Above: **Penns, 4 August 1962**. The Midland Railway line from Castle Bromwich to Walsall and Wolverhampton was perhaps a bit of a backwater, seeing local passenger services and freights, but was useful as a diversionary route and to relieve pressure on other lines. On Mondays to Fridays in the summer, the Manchester-Bournemouth 'Pines Express' used the main ex-LNW route between Wolverhampton and Birmingham New Street, but on Saturdays it took the Midland line from Wolverhampton to Walsall and Castle Bromwich, thence Lawley Street Junction and Camp Hill to King's Norton, so avoiding New Street altogether. Loco change was done at Walsall, with two engines – one for the 'Pines' and one for the following relief train – coming light from Saltley shed. On this particular date, the two locos were 'Peak' diesel D125 for the 'Pines' and 'Jubilee' 4-6-0 45648 *Hawkins* for the relief. 45648 is seen with its train, 1097, including coaches from Liverpool, going through Penns station heading for Castle Bromwich. *R J Buckley*

Below: **Water Orton**. A busy scene as Caprotti 44744 of Bristol Barrow Road shed approaches the station with an up express, while a 4-4-0 is on the down passenger line and the freight lines are also occupied. *B J Miller collection*

Left, above: **Water Orton**. The station looks more tranquil in this undated view, possibly a Sunday as there is a ballast train parked on one line. This is actually the second station here. The first opened on 16 May 1842. However, in an attempt to speed up its services, the MR built a cut off line which went from just west of the first station for almost four miles to meet the original B&D line at Kingsbury Station Junction. When this direct line opened – from 22 March 1909 for goods and on 3 May for passengers – so did the new Water Orton station, 220 yards west of the old one. Being built in a completely different era, a different design was used to that at Castle Bromwich. As the passenger lines were the two centre ones, an island platform was built with steps down from the brick building on the Minworth Road. *Stations UK*

Left, centre: **Water Orton, 1956**. 44814 brings a down express from Derby across the station junction. The line to Whitacre and Leicester is on the right, while a fast fitted van freight waits for the right away onto the Derby road at Goods Line Junction. 44814 has travelled along the direct route from Kingsbury constructed by the Midland Railway in 1909, which were designated the fast lines, with the slow lines being those via Whitacre. *R S Carpenter collection*

Left, below: **Water Orton, 8 May 1954**. With the cooling towers of Hams Hall power station in the background, 'Jubilee' 4-6-0 45699 *Galatea* uses the fast lines as it approaches Water Orton on a down Bristol express. Although the cut-off was only a mile and a quarter shorter than the line through Whitacre, it enabled the junctions at Water Orton and Kingsbury to be taken at higher speeds, as well as separating fast and slow trains. *Peter Glenn*

REGULAR FREIGHTS FROM / THROUGH BIRMINGHAM ON THE DERBY LINE UP TRAINS SEPTEMBER 1960 TO JUNE 1961

CLASS	DAYS	TIME	FROM	TO	NOTES
D	MX	12.5am	WATER ORTON	NOTTINGHAM	
F	MX	P12.3am	LANDOR STREET JC	BRANSTON	8.40pm ex Gloucester
J	MX	12.5am	BROMFORD BRIDGE	ALDRIDGE JC	Via Park Jc
F	MX	12.35am	WWH UP	EGGINTON JC	Empties
D	MX	1.10am	WATER ORTON	DERBY	7.0pm ex Bristol
E	MO	1.40am	WATER ORTON	NOTTINGHAM	A
E	MX	1.0am	LAWLEY STREET	BRENT LWS	A
E	MX	2.0am	WATER ORTON	PETERBOROUGH	A
E	MX	1.55am	WWH UP	BEESTON	Empties
F	MX	P2.7am	LANDOR STREET JC	SPONDON	8.0pm ex Didcot
E	MO	2.30am	WATER ORTON	HUNSLET	
E	MX	2.15am	LAWLEY STREET	NOTTINGHAM	
H	MO	2.40am	WATER ORTON	SHEFFIELD	
H	MX	2.30am	WWH UP	BEESTON	A Empties
F	MX	2.55am	WATER ORTON	EGGINTON JC	Empties
H	MX	3.30am	WWH UP	HUNSLET	
D	MX	3.25am	WWH UP	MASBORO	Empties
E	M-S	3.50am	WATER ORTON	CARLISLE	STOKER 9F
D	MSX	4.5am	WWH UP	WEASTE	Via Park Jc Empties
E	MX	5.0am	WWH UP	TOTON	
H	MX	5.10am	WWH UP	CHADDESDEN	
H	MX	6.0am	WATER ORTON	TAMWORTH	
F	M-S	5.45am	WWH UP	HUGGLESCOTE	A Empties 6.25am MO
E	M-S	6.45am	WWH UP	TOTON	
J	SX	6.25am	LAWLEY STREET	WHITACRE JC	
F	MO	7.15am	WWH UP	BLACKWELL	Empties
H	M-S	8.38am	WATER ORTON	WHITEMOOR	Empties
F	M-S	8.50am	WWH UP	TOTON	A
H	M-S	9.15am	WWH UP	MEASHAM	Empties
F	M-S	9.42am	WATER ORTON	BURTON	A Empties
H	M-S	9.50am	WATER ORTON	WELLINGBORO'	
F	SX	9.55am	WWH UP	KINGSBURY	A
H	MSX	10.55am	WWH UP	BEESTON	Empties
H	SX	11.0am	DUDDESTON	ARLEY COLLIERY	Empties
F	MX	11.50am	WATER ORTON	ROWSLEY	A Empties
E	M-S	P11.22am	LANDOR STREET JC	TOTON	
J	M-S	12.5pm	WWH UP	CORBY	7.25am ex Westerleigh
H	M-S	P12.42pm	LANDOR STREET JC	WATER ORTON	A SO 12.30pm
D	SX	1.0pm	WATER ORTON	CHADDESDEN	12.5pm ex Selly Oak
E	SX	1.15pm	WATER ORTON	BEESTON	
H	SX	1.15pm	WATER ORTON	OVERSEAL	
F	SX	1.45pm	WWH UP	NUNEATON	Empties
F	SX	P1.48pm	LANDOR STREET JC	WATER ORTON	A
K	SX	P1.55pm	LANDOR STREET JC	WATER ORTON	1.20pm ex Bournville
D	SO	P2.3pm	LANDOR STREET JC	WATER ORTON	1.25pm ex Longbridge
C	M-S	2.25pm	WATER ORTON	NORMANTON	8.50am ex Bristol
F	MX	2.45pm	WWH UP	CHADDESDEN	Empties
F	M-S	3.0pm	WWH UP	LITTLE EATON	Empties
J	SX	3.25pm	WWH JC	KINGSBURY	
C	FX	P3.31pm	LANDOR STREET JC	WATER ORTON	2.0pm ex Evesham
C	M-S	4.45pm	WATER ORTON	GLASGOW	
C	M-S	4.55pm	WATER ORTON	CARLISLE	STOKER 9F
C	SX	5.10pm	WATER ORTON	HUNSLET	SO Class D at 5.5pm
E	M-S	5.10pm	LAWLEY STREET	ROWSLEY	Class D ex Water Orton
H	SX	5.40pm	WATER ORTON	BURTON	
J	SO	5.30pm	WWH UP	KINGSBURY	Empties
F	SX	6.5pm	WWH UP	DESFORD	A Empties
D	SO	6.0pm	LAWLEY STREET	ST PANCRAS	A
C	SX	P6.39pm	DUDDESTON RD JC	DRINGHOUSES	2.55pm ex Bristol
E	M-S	6.35pm	WWH UP	TOTON	Empties
D	M-S	P7.48pm	LANDOR STREET JC	WATER ORTON	4.40pm ex Hinksey
F	M-S	7.0pm	WWH UP	BRANSTON	Empties
H	SO	7.40pm	WATER ORTON	BEESTON	
H	SX	7.35pm	WWH UP	KINGSBURY	Empties
C	SO	8.30pm	WATER ORTON	LEICESTER	A
C	SX	8.0pm	LAWLEY STREET	BRENT	A
E	SX	8.15pm	LAWLEY STREET	WHITEMOOR	A
D	SO	P8.45pm	DUDDESTON RD JC	HUNSLET LANE	4.48pm ex Bristol
F	M-S	P8.47pm	LANDOR STREET JC	WATER ORTON	6.35pm ex Gloucester
H	M-S	8.50pm	WATER ORTON	YORK	
C	M-S	9.15pm	LAWLEY STREET	NOTTINGHAM	
C	SX	9.5pm	LAWLEY STREET	WHITEMOOR	A
F	SO	P9.13pm	LANDOR STREET JC	WATER ORTON	5.30pm ex Bristol
D	M-S	9.40pm	WWH UP	STOCKINGFORD	A Empties
J	SX	9.30pm	LAWLEY STREET	ROWSLEY	
E	M-S	9.45pm	LAWLEY STREET	NORMANTON	Class E ex Water Orton
C	M-S	9.55pm	LAWLEY STREET	HUNSLET	
C	SX	10.15pm	WWH UP	ROWSLEY	
J	SX	10.15pm	WATER ORTON	BESCOT	Via Park Jc
E	SX	10.25pm	COLESHILL	LEICESTER	A
F	SX	10.50pm	LANDOR STREET JC	OVERSEAL	Empties
K	SX	P10.40pm	LAWLEY STREET	WATER ORTON	9.45pm ex Longbridge
C	SO	10.45pm	WATER ORTON	SHEFFIELD	
H	SX	11.10pm	LANDOR STREET JC	CHADDESDEN	7.27pm ex Hinksey
D	SO	P10.45pm	LANDOR STREET JC	WATER ORTON	
E	SX	10.55pm	WATER ORTON	DERBY	
H	SO	11.20pm	WWH UP	TOTON	
H	SX	11.20pm	WWH UP	BRANSTON	Empties
F	SO	11.20pm	WATER ORTON	TOTON	Empties
F	SX	11.27pm	LANDOR STREET JC	DERBY	7.0pm ex Bristol
D	M-S	P11.27pm	LANDOR STREET JC	DERBY	
E	M-S	11.30pm	LAWLEY STREET	SHEFFIELD	

PLUS many local trip / yard transfer workings and light engine movements

P passing time   A onto Nuneaton line at Whitacre

Coleshill, formerly Forge Mills. The Birmingham & Derby Junction Railway built a line from Water Orton to Whitacre Junction in 1842 when Forge Mills station was opened, about one and a half miles from Water Orton. Called 'Forge Mills (For Coleshill)' from 1849 to 1904, it became just Coleshill in 1923. The top picture shows the station in Midland Railway days, while the bottom view is from 8 March 1956, looking towards Whitacre. The signal box dates from 1939, replacing an earlier one adjacent to the up platform.

R M Casserley

Whitacre Junction, 16 April 1964. Highly important industrial developments took place in the triangle formed by the Water Orton to Kingsbury direct and Water Orton-Whitacre-Kingsbury lines. A large electricity generating station was opened in 1929 at Hams Hall by Birmingham Corporation; in post-war years, two more generating plants were brought into use, making it the largest power station in Europe according to some accounts. The complex had a big internal railway system – in the mid-1960s, there were 10 steam locos allocated, with between 6 and 8 in use everyday. Naturally this provided a lot of traffic for BR. There was access into Hams Hall from both Coleshill and Whitacre. In the top photo, an unidentified 8F hauls a load of empty coal wagons out of Hams Hall, while looking the other way shows another 8F, 48315, passing Whitacre station with a coal train. The power stations all closed in the early 1990s; the area is now used for freight distribution and is still rail connected. *R J Essery collection; R J Buckley*

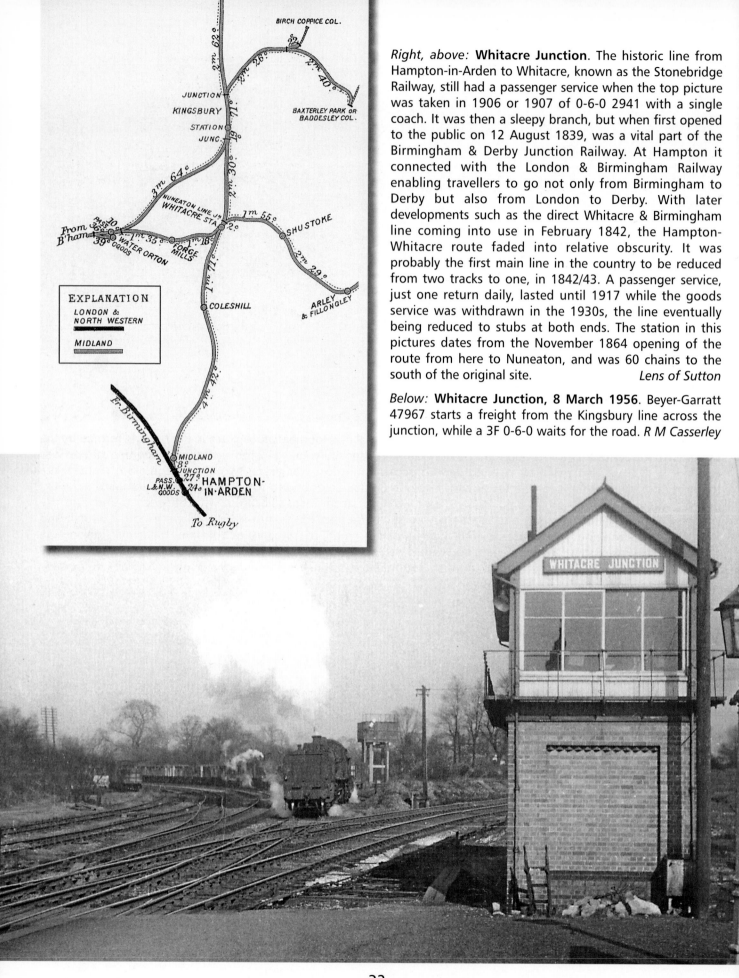

Right, above: **Whitacre Junction.** The historic line from Hampton-in-Arden to Whitacre, known as the Stonebridge Railway, still had a passenger service when the top picture was taken in 1906 or 1907 of 0-6-0 2941 with a single coach. It was then a sleepy branch, but when first opened to the public on 12 August 1839, was a vital part of the Birmingham & Derby Junction Railway. At Hampton it connected with the London & Birmingham Railway enabling travellers to go not only from Birmingham to Derby but also from London to Derby. With later developments such as the direct Whitacre & Birmingham line coming into use in February 1842, the Hampton-Whitacre route faded into relative obscurity. It was probably the first main line in the country to be reduced from two tracks to one, in 1842/43. A passenger service, just one return daily, lasted until 1917 while the goods service was withdrawn in the 1930s, the line eventually being reduced to stubs at both ends. The station in this pictures dates from the November 1864 opening of the route from here to Nuneaton, and was 60 chains to the south of the original site. *Lens of Sutton*

Below: **Whitacre Junction, 8 March 1956.** Beyer-Garratt 47967 starts a freight from the Kingsbury line across the junction, while a 3F 0-6-0 waits for the road. *R M Casserley*

Below: **Coleshill, renamed Maxstoke**. The only intermediate station between Hampton and Whitacre was at Coleshill. When Forge Mills between Water Orton and Whitacre was renamed Coleshill in July 1923, this one became Maxstoke, though of course it had already lost its passenger service – and the goods service ceased in May 1939 enabling complete closure.

Above: **24 September 1920.** There was a timber bridge over the River Blythe on the Hampton side of Coleshill station. It was removed when contractors tore up the tracks across it in 1952. *R S Carpenter collection*

Below: **Hampton, c.1880.** This portrait shows the station when it was part of the LNWR. The generous provision of platforms and buildings give a hint of its important status in earlier years. A one-time station clerk here, James Allport, rose through the ranks to become the very distinguished General Manager of the Midland Railway. *Clinker Views, Brunel University Transport Collection*

Above: **Hampton-in-Arden**. The old loco shed and works, dating from the opening of the line, became a timber yard. Twelve 2-2-2 passenger engines and two 0-4-2 goods locos formed the stock of the B&D, whose Locomotive Superintendent was Matthew Kirtley. He later went on to become the first incumbent of that post on the Midland Railway, from 1844 to 1873. *RCHS*

Below: **Hampton-in-Arden, c.1930**. On 1 September 1884 the LNWR opened a replacement station a few hundred yards to the west and two years later renamed it 'Hampton-in-Arden'. This view is towards Birmingham. *Stations UK*

35

Kingsbury-Whitacre line, 21 September 1931. The LMS Garratts were introduced to replace the double-heading of coal trains, as exemplified here by 3F 3729 and 4F 4432 making for Whitacre. This part of Warwickshire had a number of collieries, providing steady traffic for the lines in the area.

Gordon Coltas

Above: **Kingsbury, 8 March 1956**. Saltley shed had a good allocation of 'Crab' 2-6-0s for the kind of duty shown here, with 42791 passing through the station on a Birmingham-bound class 'D' express freight. Some freights, including this one, used the direct line to Water Orton. Kingsbury was one of the stations opened in 1839 and a passenger service was maintained until March 1968. About a mile north of the station were Kingsbury Branch Sidings and a Midland Railway branch to Baddesley Colliery. *R M Casserley*

Below: **Wilnecote, 1970**. Next station along the line was this quiet wayside one, opened in May 1842 as Wilnecote & Fazeley, the name being shortened in 1904. But the area has built up enough in recent years for the station to still be open with a good local service. *Stations UK*

Cliff Sidings, 16 August 1953. 'Jubilee' 45699 *Galatea*, seen approaching Water Orton in an earlier photo, was involved in a traumatic derailment between Wilnecote and Kingsbury. Luckily no-one died and only two people needed hospital treatment, even though the train, the 9.28am from Bradford to Bristol, carried over 450 passengers. The Ministry of Transport enquiry concluded that the accident was caused due to the engine 'hunting' on uneven track. A relief train arrived just two hours after the accident to take passengers away.

Perrin & Harrisons Sidings, 20 May 1963. This is the end of the up and down loops giving a quadruple line section from just north of Wilnecote station. 'Jubilee' 45597 *Barbados* of 55A Leeds Holbeck shed heads a fitted freight past the 14-lever framed signal box about half-a-mile north of Wilnecote station. The tall signal visible had a lower repeater arm.
J W Ellson

Above: **Tamworth High Level**. This station opened with the line on 12 August 1839 – though 'High Level' was not added to the name until 1924. A wet day sees a down express passing through behind a 'Black Five'. While a freight goes north, a loco can be glimpsed adjacent to the north-to-west curve opened in June 1847 linking the Derby-Birmingham line with the West Coast Main Line at the LNWR station. A 1921 plan shows there was to be a north-to-east curve as well, but this was never laid.

Stations UK

Below: **Tamworth High Level, 27 June 1925**. Early LMS days and a typical Midland double-headed express with Johnson 1P 'Spinner' 4-2-2 644 piloting 2P 4-4-0 498 start away for the north. While there were still 43 Singles in service at the Grouping in January 1923, the last was withdrawn in 1928. The roof of the brand-new High Level signal box, not opened until August this year, is visible above the train – it replaced two boxes, North and South. On the right, a brake van and wagons stand on the link line to the Low Level.

W L Good

Above: **Tamworth station**. The LNWR opened for business on 15 September 1847. The splendid edifice in this delightful view before the intrusion of motor vehicles was on the down side of the LNWR Low Level. It was used for both the LNWR and Midland Railway passengers and each has its own notice board outside. On the extreme right is the first floor connection to the MR platforms. As only local trains stopped on the Low Level, loops were built for these, leaving the fast lines clear for non-stop trains.

Below: **Tamworth station, c.1959**. The replacement building bears the legend 'Trent Valley Station' – and there are no horse-drawn carriages, but a Ford 'Consul' car which could be regarded as a classic today. In 1962 a new station opened here along with the electrification of the Trent Valley line. This necessitated lifting the High Level lines and platforms 2 feet to allow clearance for the overhead equipment. All four platforms on the Low and High Levels were lengthened to accommodate mail trains.   *A W V Mace collection / R S Carpenter collection*

Tamworth Low Level. Tamworth was a mecca for trainspotters in steam days, with the Birmingham-Derby line crossing the West Coast Main Line making it a busy place for observations. Tamworth had always been a stopping place for mail coaches before the coming of railways – it remained a very important station for Royal Mail, with seven Travelling Post Office trains transferring 2000 bags of mail between High and Low Level via a lift every night, employing 20 people. The most important of the services were those from Euston to Aberdeen and Bristol to Newcastle. The lift tower can be seen above the trains in these two pictures. The first depicts a down Carlisle express with LNW 'Prince of Wales' 4-6-0 145. The second is virtually the same view, but in 1956, and has Stanier Pacific 46249 *City of Sheffield* storming through with the down 'Mid-Day Scot'.   *LGRP; Rex Conway collection*

Above: **Tamworth water troughs, c.1963**. Just under a mile north of Tamworth station near Wigginton were these water troughs, 25 chains in length, in use from April 1909. 45464 kicks up a spray as it heads south on a parcels train. Provision of water troughs on the Midland Railway was fairly rare, these were the only ones between Bristol and Leeds. An MR style water tank still survives in the area. *N Preedy*

Below: **Elford, 2 May 1959**. About three miles further on was Elford station, with 8F 48315 approaching on a freight from Washwood Heath. The station was called Haselour upon opening in 1850, in later years rejoicing in the names of Haselour & Elford, not to mention Elford & Haselour. *H B Priestley collection*

Above: **Elford, 1949**. Another freight passes through behind a 4F 0-6-0. The station closed to passenger and goods in March 1952, but had the distinction of reopening for goods traffic from July 1954 until November 1973. The next station north, Croxall, closed in July 1928 and photographs of it are extremely elusive. It was called Oakley & Alrewas on opening in 1840, just Oakley from 1849 and Croxall from late 1856.
Stations UK

Below: **Wichnor Junction, 1957**. Class 5 4-6-0 44839 takes a northbound summer train past the modern box, dating from 1953, replacing one built in 1899. 44839 only spent the summer of 1957 shedded at 19B, Sheffield Millhouses, but was familiar enough on the line, counting 17A Derby amongst its other allocations. On the right is the ex-LNW South Staffordshire line, from Lichfield. The LNW built a small loco shed here which lasted from 1854 until 1896.
R K Blencowe collection

Above: **Wichnor Junction, 3 June 1951**. Another 'Black Five' 44857, with the 11.0am Bradford-Bristol express, steams away from the junction onto the South Staffordshire line, diverted due to Sunday engineering works at Kettlebook, south of Tamworth. It will travel all the way to Birmingham New Street on ex-LNW lines – via Lichfield, Sutton Coldfield and Aston. This was the diversion taken by the ill-fated 12.15pm York-Bristol express on Sunday 23 January 1955 with 'Black Five' 45274 which derailed at speed at Sutton Coldfield with tragic loss of life. *T G Wassell*

Below: **Barton and Walton station, 2 May 1959**. About a mile and a half north of Wichnor Junction, 'Jubilee' 45605 *Cyprus*, with a Fowler tender, pulls a down Bristol express, which includes a good selection of ex-LNER coaches. Behind it is the 1907 replacement signal box. Events moved at such a pace during the railway heyday that the MR had only reframed the box here eleven years earlier. In the foreground is the trailing access to the 70-wagon capacity goods yard with a brick shed to the left. *H B Priestley collection*

Above: **Branston, 4 June 1962**. The state of the platforms indicate that closure was some time ago – in fact it was September 1930, probably a victim of competition from road transport, coupled with the general economic depression of the time. It was altogether a short-lived station, having only opened in October 1889. 45346 passes with a northbound express. The goods line to Branston Sidings is on the left.   *B W L Brooksbank, Initial Photographics*

Below: **Branston Junction, 10 April 1965**. A view from a passing down train afford a glimpse of the sidings with a freight waiting to depart. At the other end of the sidings was the curve, opened in 1863, giving trains access to the Burton-Leicester line. There was a short branch opened in 1918 here at the Junction for the National Machine Gun Factory. In 1921 the branch was renamed the Crosse & Blackwell Siding and the factory then produced – Branston Pickle. This was short lived, closing in 1925, although the name still survives to this day. After flirtation with silk manufacture it became the Central Ordnance Depot from 1937 supplying military clothing and equipment, until closure by the MOD in 1975.   *R J Essery collection*

Above: **Gresley, 1949**. Connecting to the Birmingham-Derby route was the 31-miles-long Burton-Leicester line. Gresley station was nearly five miles from Burton, having a fairly respectable service – nine trains each way on weekdays, with two on Sundays in 1955/56. Passenger services continued until September 1964. The line connected with a number of collieries and freight traffic was always more important than passenger. In the late 1950s a coal fired power station was opened at Drakelow, about a mile and a half from Burton along this line. A new triangular junction enabled it to be supplied with coal from both directions without the need for reversing.   *Stations UK*

Below: **Swadlincote, 1951**. The original station was on a line which branched off around a mile and a half west of Gresley, but when the Woodville extension was built, looping back round to join the Burton-Leicester line nearly a mile and a half east of Gresley, it closed and a new station built. This closed to daily passenger service in October 1947, but excursion trains continued to call.   *Stations UK*

Above: **Burton-on-Trent, Leicester Junction, 30 May 1960**. The Birmingham-Derby line is straight ahead, while the one to Leicester goes off left. Leicester Junction signal box is on the right, with the Midland loco shed adjacent. On the left is Leicester Junction Sidings Junction signal box and lines to Dale Street. In the background is part of the Crown Maltings. Deeley 0-4-0T 41536 hauls a few vans along the down goods line. Rule 153 stated that, as long as there was a lamp hanging from the last vehicle, up to 35 wagons could be tripped between Wetmore sidings and Leicester Junction in clear weather!

R C Riley

The allocation at 17B Burton at 1 January 1948 (111 locos)

40364	41536	42768	43582	43938	44166	44482	47257	58130
40395		42846	43608	43972	44170	44526	47464	58160
40432	41718	42898	43619	43976	44171	44527	47641	58186
40435	41770		43623	43991	44226	44528	47643	58221
40456	41839	43188	43709	44002	44265	44551		58222
40500	41859	43214	43815	44035	44270	44597	51217	58256
40525	41865	43244		44046	44295	44599	51235	58258
40526	41878	43247	43837	44047	44316	44600		58263
40631		43256	43847	44048	44428		56020	58284
40633	42336	43286	43892	44087	44429	47000		58297
		43306	43916	44100	44433		58057	58304
41516	42757	43340	43917	44124	44434	47231	58060	
41523	42763	43388	43919	44143	44435	47233	58087	
41533	42767	43395	43930	44156	44436	47253		

Above: **Burton-on-Trent loco shed, 12 August 1934**. Three main-line railways had loco sheds at Burton; this is the Midland's, displaying some fairly ancient motive power. The 2-4-2T 1459 is ex-North Staffordshire Railway 61; the NSR had its own loco shed in Burton at one time, the third being for the LNWR.

Although the MR had various small-scale locomotive servicing facilities here since 1847, it was in 1870 that a new roundhouse shed south of the station adjacent to Leicester Junction and centred around a 42' turntable was opened. Next to it an engineman's lodgings house was built in 1873. The shed was coded '2' in the MR system. With some foresight, this No.1 shed was set back from the main line so that when in 1892 another roundhouse, this time with a 50' turntable, was opened, it was slotted in between the two. With larger engines arriving after the Grouping in 1923, the LMS replaced the turntables: 57' for No.1 shed and a 55' version in No.2 shed. In 1935 it was recoded 17B, during steam's demise it changed to 16F, becoming a sub-shed of Nottingham, until closure in 1968.

Below: **Burton shed, 17B, 1960**. When BR came into existence in 1948, there were 111 locos allocated here. A glimpse inside the roundhouse reveals two Deeley 0-4-0Ts, 41532 and 41536, which were utilised, along with various other small tanks, for shunting wagons for the brewery traffic. The Ivatt 2-6-2T on the left appears to be stored, probably because it used to work the 'Tutbury Jenny' service which ceased during 1960.   *Rail Archive Stephenson*

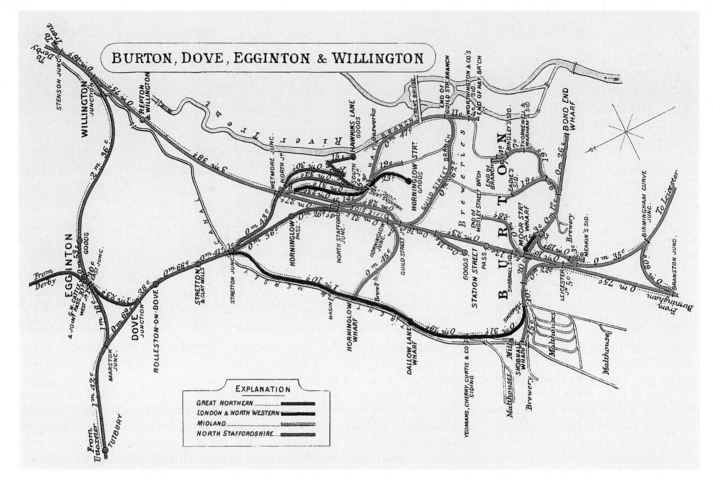

Burton was a mass of railways, mostly serving the brewing industry, some shunted by main line locos and others by the breweries' own engines, which were noted for their very smart appearance.

Not shown on this map was the Midland Railway-owned Burton & Ashby Light Railway, an electrified rural tramway of 3'6" gauge worked by open-top double-deck cars, painted in dark maroon and cream adorned with the Midland Railway coat-of-arms. C Hamilton Ellis described it as 'a quaint little line, switchbacking across the fields, though some of its more urban environs were rather repellent'. Bus competition saw its demise with the last day of operations being 19 February 1927.

Burton-on-Trent, 1967. These three views show parts of the Midland Railway's Bond End, and Shobnall branches which were connected up and ran under the Birmingham-Derby main line, south of Burton station, with Shobnall to the west, Bond End to the east.

Dale Street Junction, *left below*, shows the tracks coming in from Wellington Street, *below*, on the Shobnall branch and heading towards Uxbridge Street, *above*, on the Bond End branch. The view at Uxbridge Street Junction is looking ahead towards Bond End Wharf; this section was closed in March 1964. The line to the left is the Duke Street branch. The picture at Wellington Street shows the signal box opened in 1901. The Shobnall branch originally ran from the south end of Burton station, opened in 1873, but in November 1876 a new curve was laid in from Leicester Junction onto the branch.

Scrimgeour Collection, Signalling Record Society

Shobnall Branch, 31 August 1957. Johnson 0-6-0T 41878 is engaged in shunting, while 4F 44599 is on a freight in the background. The LNWR had a connection at Shobnall Junction for their Dallow Lane branch, which actually also connected with the North Staffordshire Railway line from Stoke-on-Trent at Stretton Junction. The view from the footbridge looking towards the canal shows Shobnall Road on the right as it rises up and over the LNWR branch. Behind the engine are some wagons for the Canal Wharf; a line led from this across the canal to Marston, Thompson & Evershed's Brewery. On the left, controlled by Shobnall Crossing box, were connections to Shobnall Maltings, part of the vast Bass empire. The Shobnall Maltings eventually became the last Burton branch, closing in October 1979. Note the well-used foot crossing and the well tended allotments.
P J Shoesmith

52

Above: **Burton-on-Trent, 5 July 1952**. The 7.54am Worcester-York enters with two 4-4-0s – 2P 40364 and Compound 41143. Station South box is in the background. Some interesting dining and kitchen cars are stored in the Ind Coope bottling plant siding on the right. The Mosley Street branch is on the far left. The Shobnall branch and Bond Street branch lines were under the main line beyond the signal box. Originally there was a branch of the Trent & Mersey canal to serve the brewing industries east of the town and the main line passed over it by a drawbridge. However, following an accident in 1846, a permanent bridge was built. In the early 1870s the MR bought the canal, filled it in, and connected up the Shobnall and Bond Street branches. To achieve this, not only did the line underneath have to dip down, but the main line had to be raised giving a small hump. *R J Buckley, Initial Photographics*

Below: **Burton-on-Trent, c.1910**. The style of the station at platform level is displayed here, while a down passenger train waits to depart. It opened in April 1883, replacing the 1839 station and was about 150 yards to the south of the earlier one. The former level crossing was replaced by an overbridge. The line through the station was quadrupled; on the outside were goods lines with passenger lines inside, flanking an island platform. There was a bay at either end. A two-storey set of substantial buildings were at platform level and passengers accessed the platforms down steps from the road level entrance. *Stations UK*

Above: **Burton-on-Trent, exterior, 5 September 1962.** A nice period piece from the 1960s. When it opened in April 1883, this station was described as 'early English style, partly timbered'. A new station replaced this one in 1971. The name was plain 'Burton' until 1903 when it became 'Burton-on-Trent'. The town's 1878 Charter was for 'Burton upon Trent' – a fact overlooked by the railway companies and many others. *B W L Brooksbank*

Below: **Burton-on-Trent, 1960.** 9F 92152 heads a freight towards Birmingham, and two trains are at the station, the left-hand one being in the bay. There was a service from Burton to Leicester at this date which was mainly DMU, but with the occasional steam-hauled passenger. The box is Station South. *Midland Railway Trust*

Burton-on-Trent, 18 June 1957. A couple of scenes at the south end, as seen from Moor Street Crossing. Saltley's 44814 departs on a special from the down platform. The curvature of the main lines around the island platform necessitated a 30mph speed restriction for trains not booked to stop here. This 'kink' still persists today and still causes non-stop trains to slow down. Burton's own 'Crab' 42818 appears to be shunting, evidenced by the lack of a brake van. A dozen 'Crabs' were allocated to Burton in 1957, including all five fitted in 1953 with Reidinger rotary poppet valve gear, of which 42818 is one. Their workings included fast fitted beer trains. *B W L Brooksbank, Initial Photographics*

Above: **Burton-on-Trent, 5 September 1962**. The 'Crabs' were largely replaced by 'Jubilees' which were seeking a new role following dieselisation of many express passenger turns. Burton got quite an allocation of these 3-cylinder 4-6-0s, including 45620 *North Borneo* shown here on a short fitted freight. The Burton 'Jubilees' did manage some passenger work, including reliefs and substituting for failed diesels. *B W L Brooksbank, Initial Photographics*

Below: **Burton-on-Trent, June 1958**. One of Burton's famous breweries advertises itself and its products on the right, as 3F 43763 of 17A Derby trundles a freight past the station on the down slow line. Station North signal box is on the left. *B J Miller collection*

Burton-on-Trent, 30 May 1960. The 'Tutbury Jenny' Rail Motor awaits departure in the up bay with Ivatt 2-6-2T 41277. (The rail motor arrangement allowed the driver to operate the engine from the footplate or from the end compartment of the coach.) This service ceased shortly after, on and from 13 June. It was a short journey, just ten minutes for the five and a quarter miles to Tutbury. But there had been eight trains each way on weekdays and even two on Sundays. The line was basically a North Staffordshire Railway branch, connecting at Tutbury with its Stoke-on-Trent to Derby service. There had been three intermediate stations, but their passenger service was withdrawn on and from 1 January 1949.

R C Riley

Main beer trains starting from Burton 1960 / 61

Class	Days	Train
C	MO	1.20pm Horninglow Bridge-Westerleigh Sidings
C	SX	4.20pm Horninglow Bridge-Bristol West Depot
C	SX	6.50pm Horninglow Bridge-Dock Junction, London
C	M-S	8.12pm Horninglow Bridge-Washwood Heath No. 2
C	SX	11.10pm Horninglow Bridge-Wigston Sidings
C	SX	8.23pm Wetmore Sidings-Carlisle
C	MO	9.10pm Wetmore Sidings-Niddrie
C	SX	6.10pm Hawkins Lane-York
C	SX	6.55pm Hawkins Lane-Colwick
C	SX	8.45pm Horninglow Yard-Mold Junction
C	SX	9.28pm Burton Goods-Swansea

Other trains not originating at Burton also carried beer

Right, above: **Burton-on-Trent, Bass Brewery Railway.** So extensive were railways in Burton it was claimed that in 1951 they covered nearly one-quarter of all the land in use in the county borough for commercial and industrial purposes. With Guild Street No 2 signal box in the distance, a loco takes its van train past the Bass loco shed. *David Lawrence*

Right, below: **Burton-on-Trent, Ind Coope & Allsopp.** One of the most modern steam locos in the brewing industry was this 4-wheel geared Sentinel, one of two acquired post-war, posing with a full crew complement. Both had gone by 1961, one being sold to a colliery and the other scrapped. *R T Russell*

Below: **Burton-on-Trent, Bass Brewery Railway.** Immaculate Neilson Reid 0-4-0ST built in 1899, No. 10 in the Bass locomotive fleet, stands close to Allsopp's Crossing box with the Directors' 4-wheel saloon carriage. The loco was withdrawn in May 1963 and was towed up through Derby in a goods train for scrap with other locos from Bass. *David Lawrence*

Above: **Burton-on-Trent, 26 May 1959**. It almost goes without saying that Burton beer trains, usually class C, express freights, ran to regular schedules and to all parts. 'Crab' 2-6-0s were the favoured motive power for many of these trains for some years and 42763 has the 6.50pm departure for London from Old Dixie Sidings, Horninglow Bridge. Sturdy wooden beer barrels were conveyed in open wagons as well as vans.   *R C Riley*

Below: **Burton-on-Trent, ex-LNW shed, Horninglow Junction, 3 May 1936**. This was quite a substantial structure, still in use for many years after the Grouping. It opened at Hawkins Lane in 1883 as a four road shed. Roofing problems with the northlight style saw it replaced with a standard LMS type roof in 1946. The shed closed in September 1960. Locos identified in this view are: ex-MR 3F 3608; ex-LNWR G1 0-8-0 9211; ex-LNWR 1F 0-6-0T 1823.

L W Perkins, Kidderminster Railway Museum

Above: **Burton-on-Trent, Hawkins Lane Sidings, 26 May 1959**. K3 2-6-0 61870 passes the box with a fitted freight as it starts to climb up over the main line and head for Egginton Junction. Class 'C' beer trains for BR Eastern and North Eastern Regions which took this route included the 6.10pm to York and 6.55pm to Colwick, both starting from Hawkins Lane. There had been a separate ex-Great Northern Railway line over the main line, but it closed in 1954. At the same time the box seen in this picture was renamed from Burton South Junction. *R C Riley*

Below: **Burton-on-Trent, Wetmore Sidings, 26 May 1959**. These were at the northern end of Burton on both sides of the Birmingham-Derby main line. 'Jinty' 47464 hauls a trip workings on the up goods line. New Wetmore sidings on the right, up side, were probably laid around 1879-82 with a capacity for 486 wagons. This was the starting point for many northbound trains. On the down side were the earlier Old Wetmore sidings dating from the 1860s which were able to hold 245 wagons. A 3F 0-6-0 is visible. *R C Riley*

Above: **Horninglow station, 1949.** After leaving the Birmingham-Derby line at North Stafford Junction, this station on the NSR branch to Tutbury was soon reached. It closed to passenger trains on the first of January this year, no longer a calling place for the 'Tutbury Jenny'. *Stations UK*

Below: **Stretton and Clay Mills, 8 August 1959.** This ex-NSR station was also on the Tutbury branch. It closed the same date as Horninglow and the next station along, Rolleston-on-Dove. 41277 is passing the closed station propelling the 5.35pm from Tutbury to Burton. *R J Buckley, Initial Photographics*

Above: **Rolleston-on-Dove, 1949**. The neat and tranquil station still looks ready to receive passengers, sadly trains no longer called here. Not far north was Dove Junction, where the line to Tutbury went left, while another line turned right for Egginton. There was also a line direct from Tutbury to Egginton, completing the triangle.   *Stations UK*

Below: **Egginton Junction, 15 August 1959**. This had been a joint station between the Great Northern Railway and the NSR. The train has come along the Birmingham-Derby route through Burton to North Stafford Junction, then past Horninglow, Stretton and Rolleston to Dove Junction, and traversed one side of the triangle to arrive here. It will now use the ex-GNR line towards Derby with a long cross-country journey ahead before arriving at the seaside – not really a train for day-trippers.

21B Bournville shed's 4F 44463 will have brought M212, the summer Saturday 8.50am Kings Norton-Skegness, from its starting point and is a perfect example of the diagramming of freight 0-6-0s on relief passenger workings.

R J Buckley, Initial Photographics

Above: **Clay Mills, 19 April 1954.** Back on the Birmingham-Derby main line north of Burton, another 4F, 44423, of 15C Leicester, steams away on an Easter Monday excursion train from Coalville to Matlock, a relatively short distance, definitely targeted at day-trippers. The train will have come up the Leicester to Burton route. This section of the Birmingham-Derby has goods lines as well as the main lines. The building on the left, now a museum, is Clay Mills pumping station, to which effluent flowed from the Burton breweries. It was then pumped to the sewage works at Egginton by steam-powered beam engines.

P Webb

Below: **Repton and Willington, 1949.** Upon opening in 1839 this station was plain 'Willington'; it then had various name combinations before settling on the one shown. 'Alight Here for Repton School' is below the station name, indicating possibly the real reason for this station – to serve the famous public school. It closed to goods in 1964, but survived as a passenger station until March 1968.

Stations UK

Above: **Willington-Stenson Junction section, 1931.** Deeley 0-6-4T 2001, in charge of a Burton-Derby stopping passenger train, lays a smoke trail across the countryside. The signal box in the background appears to be at a junction, possibly North Stafford Junction – not the one at Burton, but the one for Egginton Junction and Tutbury.

E R Morten

Below: **Willington-Stenson Junction section, 20 May 1933.** LMS Garratt 4985 hauls a 99 wagon freight on the down with a fraction of the smoke emitted by 2001 on its 4 coaches. Again there is a signal box in the background, possibly Stenson Junction. The box-to-box distances on this stretch of line were: Willington station to North Stafford Junction 64 chains; North Stafford Junction to Stenson Junction 46 chains. Just visible on the left is the Trent & Mersey canal, bought by the North Staffordshire Railway to eliminate competition.

E R Morten

Stenson Junction, 3 October 1959. 'Black Five' 44660 powers away from the junction with the down 'Devonian'. The modern, 1954 built, signal box is in the centre distance. On the right is a coal train on the arrival line of the British Electricity Authority's Willington power station. The MR's Stenson & Weston chord to Chellaston Junction and Trent veers off to the right of the signal box.

R J Buckley, Initial Photographics

Above: **Stenson Junction, 6 May 1956**. With the Birmingham-Derby line in the background, 8F 48350 accelerates away on the Stenson & Weston section with some empty wagons for Toton. Note the brake van along the train, probably this signifies two sets of empties. *R J Buckley, Initial Photographics*

Below: **Chellaston & Swarkestone, 18 April 1954**. This station was on the line from Chellaston Junction to Melbourne Junction, part of the Derby & Melbourne route opened to passenger and goods on 1 September 1868. Although it closed to passengers on and from 22 September 1930, excursion trains continued to call and here is one doing just that. 'Crab' 42769 is in charge of this Castle Donington-Blackpool special on Easter Sunday. Looks like at least two passengers are waiting, shepherded by a BR official, while some children have turned up on the other platform to witness the exciting spectacle of a passenger train actually stopping here! *R J Buckley, Initial Photographics*

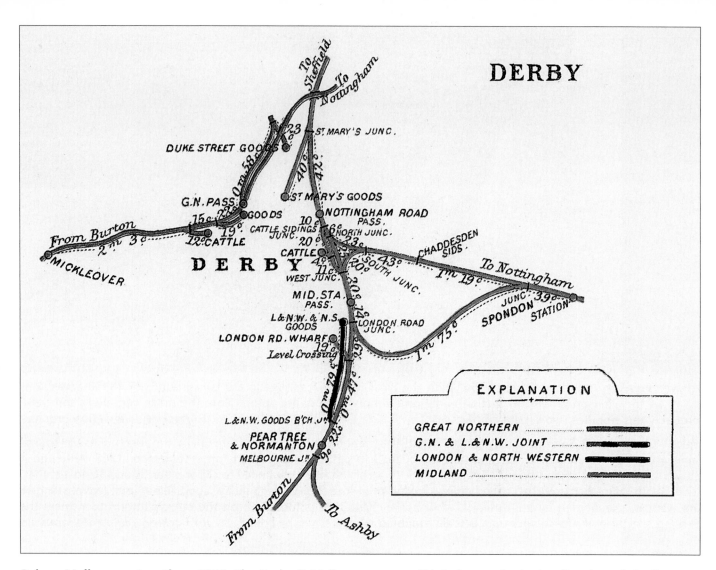

DERBY

To Sheffield
To Nottingham

St Mary's Junc.
Duke Street Goods
23
40°
42°

G.N. Pass.
St Mary's Goods
Nottingham Road Pass.
From Burton
15°
Goods
10°
North Junc.
2m 3°
19°
Cattle Sidings Junc.
16°
72 Cattle
20°
Cattle
23°
Chaddesden Sids.
Mickleover
4°
South Junc.
1m 19°
To Nottingham

DERBY
11°
West Junc.
30°
14°
Spondon
Junc.
39°
Station
Mid. Sta. Pass.
London Road Junc.
L.&N.W. & N.S. Goods
London Rd. Wharf
1m 75°
19°
Level Crossing
62°

EXPLANATION

L.&N.W. Goods B'ch Jn.
0m 79°
0m 47°
Pear Tree & Normanton
Melbourne Jn.
9°

GREAT NORTHERN
G.N. & L.&N.W. JOINT
LONDON & NORTH WESTERN
MIDLAND

From Burton
To Ashby

Below: **Melbourne Junction, 1958.** The Derby & Melbourne goes off left; interestingly the direction of the line was UP from here to Trent. The Birmingham to Derby line, which was UP to Derby, comes in from the right. Between Stenson Junction and here, three and a quarter miles, there were two goods and two passenger lines. *Stations UK*

68

Above: **Pear Tree & Normanton**. This station, only one mile from Derby station, was adjacent to Melbourne Junction and the freight, hauled by 3F 3792, appears to have crossed from the Melbourne line. Adjacent to the road bridge can be seen the booking office, complete with clock! A steep path leads to the small shelter on the down platform, with, further back, a large station name board. *LGRP*

Below: **London & North Western Junction, Derby, 20 April 1956**. At this point the pair of lines that passed through Pear Tree & Normanton station widen into six. On the up side were a pair giving access to the LNWR's goods yard at St. Andrews and its engine shed. On the down side were a pair of goods lines which by-passed Derby station to the east. Just after 2am on this day a down freight train came to grief here. Fortunately, the pointwork for the crossover was against the train and so it ran into the stop block. This saved the 24 lever frame signal box from demolition by the 'Black Five'. *Dave Harris collection*

Above: **London Road Junction, Derby, 14 September 1953**. The original 1839 Midland Counties line was at the north end of Derby station, so trains between London and the north needed to reverse. Consequently a curve just under two miles long was opened on 27 June 1867 from this junction south of the station to join the original line at Spondon Junction.

Derby designed BR Standard class 3 2-6-2T 84006 was virtually new when photographed arriving on this Burton to Derby local. Along with 84007 and 84008 it was allocated to 17B Burton, staying for about five years.

Midland Railway Trust

Below: **London Road Junction, Derby, 1960**. Three 9Fs, 92165, 92166 and 92167 were fitted with Berkley mechanical stokers and allocated to 21A Saltley for what *Trains Illustrated* called 'probably the most arduous fitted freight diagrams on British Railways'. These involved workings between Water Orton and Carlisle, manned throughout by Saltley crews on lodging turns. Trains loaded up to 50 wagons on the class 'C' freights and 55 with the class 'D'. The stokers were not a total success and all three locos had lost them by 1962. 92167 is depicted coming in from Burton with a class 'C' working.

Midland Railway Trust

London Road Junction, Derby. A couple of expresses leave Derby for Birmingham with traditional 4-4-0 power. 2P 502 heads a Bristol train in 1925 with a motley collection of stock including a horse box. Compound 41021 is depicted in April 1952 departing on a Birmingham train with the ex-LNWR and North Staffordshire Railway goods warehouse in the background. *Real Photographs; Frank Ashley*

Above: **Derby station, 1980**. The frontage is rather splendid as befits the headquarters of the Midland Railway. The station opened in May 1840 on ground at Castle Field when the North Midland Railway commenced its services, whilst the B&D shifted here from a temporary station adjoining London Road overbridge that it had used since August 1839. The Midland Counties also used the station when it started running services into Derby. In the late 1850s two storey extensions were built on either side of the entrance and, between these two blocks, a pillared wall was put up so carriages could pass through to drop off and pick up passengers. Additional platforms were added in 1867 and various alterations made in 1876. In 1893 the whole front was rebuilt using reclaimed materials, this time there were separate arrival and booking areas for first and second class passengers.   *N D Mundy*

Below: **Derby station, 16 April 1959**. 'Midland Station' is proclaimed twice on the front, to distinguish it from any other, lesser, station in Derby. The name was applied by BR in September 1950 and in 1952-54 some of the platforms were rebuilt. The road vehicles on display appear to be completely British – those were the days! And it's raining, what more could one want to complete a nostalgic picture.   *H C Casserley*

Derby Midland. Looking north, down from the footbridge that gave access to Derby Works, shows the station before the train sheds came down completely. New platform canopies – see the page 75 picture – were erected in 1954. Platform 1 is in the background. A down train is due judging by the passenger activity on platform 6, most probably for London. 4P Compound 41021, with a horse-box behind the loco, and 3P 735 attend to business. 3P 4-4-0s had been the biggest power on West of England trains until the viaduct near Wichnor was strengthened in 1924, allowing Compounds to work the line.
Author's collection

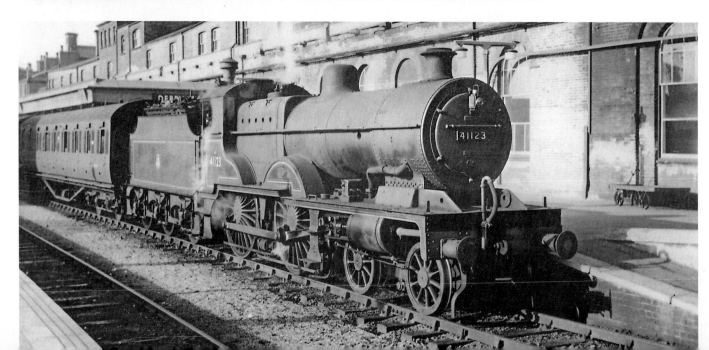

Left, above and centre: **Derby Midland**. Ex-LNER locos were seen daily at Derby on stopping trains from Lincoln via Nottingham. Two fine engines photographed on the working are D16/3 4-4-0 62571 in 1957 and ex-Great Central Robinson designed 4-6-2T 69820. *Midland Railway Trust*

Left, below: **Derby Midland, 1957**. Compound 41123 has arrived on a stopping train from Gloucester, where its home depot was Barnwood. It had only been allocated there since May 1957, previously being at Trafford Park, so was likely to have been a fairly regular sight at Derby. 41123 was withdrawn in December 1959. It was outlived by 17A Derby's own 41157, the last working Compound on BR, withdrawn in May 1960. *R S Carpenter collection*

Above: **Derby Midland, 2 October 1955**. While ex-LNER locos were everyday sights at the home of the Midland Railway, GWR motive power was not often represented. The railcars are the twin units W33W and W38W with an ordinary coach in the middle. The occasion is an enthusiasts railtour run by the 'Westminster Bank Railway Society' from and to London Paddington via Bordesley Junction, Birmingham and Burton. *R J Buckley, Initial Photographics*

Right: **Derby station 'A' box**. This was opened in 1881, just a small cabin positioned on the centre platform. It controlled the crossovers between platforms 1 & 2 and 3 & 4. 35 levers worked small semaphore signals pivoted halfway along the arms. A new box, the one seen here, replaced it during the 1950s rebuilding of the station and was nicknamed 'the cupboard under the stairs'. Two aspect colour lights replaced the semaphores, green on top of red; the box closed in July 1969. *R K Blencowe collection*

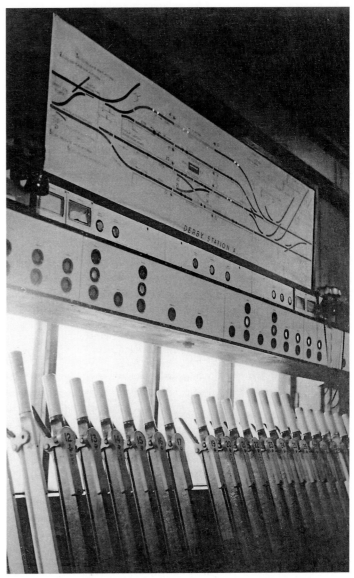

Passenger and Parcels Trains Birmingham-Derby Weekdays 8 June to 20 September 1953

Depart NEW ST	Train No.	Train	Arrive DERBY	Notes	Loco on Aug 7 1954
12.6am	P482	8.0pm Parcels Bristol-Leeds	1.20am		
1.35am	P484 SX	10.15pm Perishables Bath-Derby	2.42am		
3.0am	P486 SX	1.45pm Parcels Bristol-Derby	4.17am		
1.42am	200 MO	Birmingham-Lincoln Mails	3.3am	Starts Tamworth at 2.25am MX	
3.15am	202 SO	12.30am Bristol-Sheffield	4.22am	Runs 11 July to 22 August	
4.37am	204	1.10am Bristol-Sheffield	5.45am	Mails to Derby	
6.40am	208	6.40am Birmingham-Bradford	7.48am	Runs to Glasgow SO	
7.48am	B	7.20am Kings Norton-Derby	9.23am		
8.2am	294	8.2am Birmingham-Newcastle	8.59am		
8.35am	298 SO	7.15am Worcester-Filey Camp	9.43am	Until 5 September	44811
8.45am	300 SO	8.20am Kings Norton-Scarborough	9.50am	Until 5 September	43017
9.0am	302	7.54am Worcester-York	10.13am		41180
9.15am	212 SO	8.50am Kings Norton-Skegness	0	10.6am from Burton, then via Egginton Jc	44418
10.12am	218	7.35am Bristol-Bradford	11.3am		45682
11.0am	322 SO	8.30am Bristol-Newcastle	11.56am		45264
11.35am	304	8.30am Cardiff-Newcastle	12.39pm		45620
12.36pm	222 FSO	10.10am Bristol-Sheffield	1.32pm	Starts 19 June	45656
12.50pm	306	10.16am Bristol-Newcastle	1.36pm		45572
12.54pm	B SO	12.54pm Birmingham-Derby	2.22pm		
1.22pm	224 SO	8.5am Bournemouth-Sheffield	2.32pm	Runs 25 July to 5 September	44919
1.27pm	B	1.27pm Birmingham-Derby	2.52pm		
2.8pm S	310 SO	7.45am Paignton-Newcastle	2.58pm	Starts 4 July	44757
2.6pm	228 SO	8.40am Bournemouth-Bradford	3.8pm	Runs 4 July to 12 September	44853
2.27pm S	232 SO	8.52am Paignton-Sheffield	3.24pm	Runs to Leeds 11 July to 22 August	42703
2.40pm	238 MFO	9.55am Bournemouth-Sheffield	3.36pm	From Birmingham only MFSX	
2.53pm S	240 SO	8.55am Kingswear-Bradford	3.50pm		45561
3.6pm	240 SX	9.0am Kingswear-Bradford	4.1pm		
3.12pm S	238 SO	9.55am Bournemouth-Leeds	4.12pm		44826
3.24pm	242 SO	12.45pm Bristol-Sheffield	4.23pm	Starts 27 June	44986
3.33pm	244 SO	12.15pm Weston-S-Mare-Sheffield	4.35pm		44666
3.46pm	248 SO	10.15am Teignmouth-Bradford	5.5pm		45662
4.23pm	256 FO	11.40am Bournemouth-Derby	5.19pm		
4.26pm	254 SO	11.12am Bournemouth-Derby	5.20pm	Runs 11 July to 29 August	44035
4.36pm	314 SO	8.10am Newquay-Newcastle	5.33pm	From 27 June	45654
4.42pm	316	2.15pm Bristol-York	5.42pm		44814
4.49pm	256 SO	11.40am Bournemouth-Sheffield	5.50pm		44851
5.15pm	B	5.15pm Birmingham-Derby	6.41pm		
5.50pm	B	4.25pm Worcester-Derby	7.15pm		
6.20pm	B	6.20pm Birmingham-Derby	7.49pm		
7.10pm	268 FO	4.15pm Bristol-Derby	8.13pm		
7.17pm	268 SO	4.45pm Bristol-Derby	8.14pm	Runs 4 July-12 September	43924
7.17pm	320 SX	4.45pm Bristol-York	8.21pm		
7.31pm	320 SO	11.0am Newquay-York	8.35pm		45585
8.31pm	272 SO	10.45am Penzance-Sheffield	9.42pm		45577
9.0pm	B	9.0pm Birmingham-Derby	10.34pm		
10.11pm	324 FO	7.32pm Bristol-York	11.17pm		
10.40pm	326	7.20pm Bristol-Newcastle	11.46pm		
11.34pm	P328 SX	11.5pm Parcels Birmingham Central-York	12.51am		

S time at Saltley, train runs via Camp Hill   Loco on this train on Saturday 7 August 1954 from an RCTS traffic survey

The Midland Railway did not have a total monopoly on stations in Derby – the Great Northern Railway had one at Friargate. This opened in 1878 as part of the GNR's Derbyshire Extension. The line went on to Egginton Junction where it connected with the North Staffordshire Railway route to the Potteries, thus providing a useful alternative to the Midland. In later years, there were regular trains from Friargate to Nottingham Victoria; the passenger service west of Derby had ceased at the start of World War 2, though excursion trains, like the one depicted on page 63 of this book, still used the route.

Above: **Derby South Junction, Chaddesden Sidings, 1951**. Located approximately north-east of Derby station, various Washwood Heath and Water Orton freights started or terminated here. There were eight reception lines, seven departure and 31 marshalling sidings. Services such as the Water Orton-Carlisle trains called at St Mary's Junction, three-quarters of a mile north of Derby station, to pick up or drop off traffic for St Mary's Goods depot. 4F 44101 passes the sidings with a freight for Trent. Trains from the north for Trent and vice-versa avoid Derby station by using this section of line – one such in the early 1960s was the diesel 'Midland Pullman' set from London to Manchester.

R J Buckley, Initial Photographics

Below: **Spondon Junction, 16 September 1951**. Leaving the Birmingham-Derby route at London Road Junction is the main line for Trent, Leicester and London St Pancras, which goes via the Spondon Curve and meets the Chaddesden line at Spondon Junction. Compound 4-4-0 41040 approaches the junction on the 12.15pm Derby-Trent service.

R J Buckley, Initial Photographics

Above: **Derby, 26 August 1920.** The Birmingham & Derby Railway had its own engine shed at Derby, as did the Midland Counties Railway and North Midland Railway, which all became part of the Midland Railway. While the B&D shed was demolished after about 30 years use, the North Midland shed is the one seen here in 1920. Locos in view are stated as being; 1245; 1603; 777; 3186; 1326 and 1426. *H C Casserley*

Below: **Derby, 18 May 1932.** A mighty gathering of locos in the yard. Those on the nearest three lines appear stored, with empty tenders. 2-4-0 77 is on the left, with 0-6-0 2724 on the next road. The sheer number of 0-6-0 tender engines reflects MR motive power policy. The footbridge in the background is the one from the station to the works. *H C Casserley*

The allocation at 17A Derby at 1 January 1948 (137 locos)

40325	41000	41773	43308	43550	44031	44602	45639	58077
40383	41003	41779	43312	43572	44101	44605	45656	58090
40404	41033	41788	43315	43574	44142		45667	
40407	41036	41795	43318	43584	44177	44809		58125
40411	41055	41833	43323	43598	44195	44815	47417	58132
40416	41057	41847	43324	43658	44214	44818		58144
40426	41059		43364	43735	44263	44819	48157	58145
40482	41060	42340	43368	43745	44402	44839	48322	58148
40516	41083	42341	43370	43759	44409	44851	48390	58158
40632	41084		43402	43776	44419	44962	48404	58188
	41088	42847	43406		44420	45088	48432	58216
40711		42872	43459	43838	44430	45261	48640	58227
40734	41535	42897	43482	43839	44432	45285	48647	58230
40735				43840	44542		48654	58246
40743	41695	43191	43496	43881	44565	45585	48677	58253
40756	41726	43200	43510	43955	44566	45602		
	41754	43273	43548	44023	44601	45610	58035	

Below: **Derby Midland, 1951.** Many steam locomotives were constructed at Derby over the years and 130 of the 172 BR Standard class 5MT 4-6-0s emerged from the Works between 1951 and 1957, with boilers made at Crewe. 73002 is brand-new in this portrait taken from platform 6 with the Works in the background. 73154, equipped with Caprotti valve gear, was the last steam loco built at Derby.
T G Wassall

79

Midland Railway gradient profile of 1902.

Scale of Sections {Horizontal: 5 Miles to an inch
Vertical: 500 Feet to an inch
Datum Line is 300 Feet below Ordnance Datum
Gradients: Figures written thus "100" indicate "1 in 100" - "L" indicates "Level"
Altitudes: Indicated thus "Alt. 72·21" and denotes the height in Feet above Ordnance Datum

BIRMINGHAM

DERBY   BURTON-ON-TRENT   TAMWORTH

DERBY   AND   BIRMINGHAM   LINE   ASTON CURVE

Mileage table

Birmingham New Street to Derby Midland
41 miles 16 chains via direct line

Birmingham New Street	0.00
Saltley	2.10
Washwood Heath No.1	2.60
Castle Bromwich	5.27
Water Orton	7.49
Kingsbury	11.62
Tamworth High Level	17.27
Wichnor Junction	24.78
Burton on Trent	30.16
Stenson Junction	36.31
Derby Midland	41.16
Water Orton	0.00
Whitacre	2.64
Kingsbury	5.34
Whitacre	0.00
Hampton	6.33

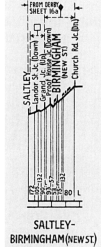

SALTLEY–
BIRMINGHAM (NEW ST.)

Acknowledgements

This volume has been most difficult to assemble due to the absolute dearth of material for some key locations such as the sidings at Lawley Street, Washwood Heath, Hams Hall and Water Orton. Patience was not rewarded and this is probably as good as it gets in those places! Pictures of other features have been similarly elusive: goods warehouses at Burton spring to mind and Croxall station may as well have never existed!

There were, however, several sources of inspiration which helped redress the balance: the *Birmingham New Street* series by Richard Foster; *Brewery Railways of Burton-on-Trent* by Cliff Shepherd; and *The Midland Railway - A Chronology* by John Gough. Special mention must go to the volunteers of Kidderminster Railway Museum, particularly Audie Baker, for their enthusiasm, and the publisher, Stephen Mourton, for his continuous support and friendship. Members of the Midland Railway Society have been more than generous with their time, knowledge and expertise, especially Dave 'King of Signalling' Harris. Public libraries have been a great source of information, chiefly the local studies sections at Birmingham, Burton and Derby as well as the latter's Industrial Museum.

Books, magazines and articles too numerous to mention were consulted as well as ideas and accounts in the booklets of a large number of railway and allied transport societies.

While every effort has been made to obtain permission from owners of copyright materials contained herein, the publisher would like to apologise for any omissions and will be pleased to incorporate missing acknowledgements in any future editions.